THE
MOUNTAIN
Pine Beetle

TINY BUT
Mighty

THE MOUNTAIN Pine Beetle

TINY BUT MIGHTY

BY KAY Turnbaugh

WITH ILLUSTRATIONS BY DAVID BROOKS

PRUETT

PRUETT PUBLISHING COMPANY
BOULDER, COLORADO
pruettpublIshing.com

ACKNOWLEDGEMENTS

This book owes its existence to a Continuing Education class I took at the University of Colorado. Our teacher, Sean McCollum, and my writing group that evolved from that class helped with many initial drafts. Sheryl Costello, an entomologist with the U.S. Forest Service, worked with me on the details of mountain pine beetle life. Thanks to my editor, Theresa Howell, and her "bug expert" husband, Brian, and his friends, and to publisher Jim Pruett. Designer Katie Jennings helped bring the manuscript alive, and illustrator David Brooks added the sparkle with his insightful, funny, and eloquent drawings.

©2011 by Kay Turnbaugh
Illustrations ©2011 by David Brooks

Address all inquiries to:
Pruett Publishing Company, PO Box 2140, Boulder, CO 80306, pruettpublishing.com

ISBN 978-0-87108-958-8

Library of Congress Cataloging-in-Publication Data

Turnbaugh, Kay.
The mountain pine beetle : tiny but mighty / by Kay Turnbaugh ; with illustrations by David Brooks.
    p. cm.
Includes index.
Summary: "Describes the mountain pine beetle and how it has caused an epidemic of dead trees in the Rocky Mountains"--Provided by publisher.
ISBN 978-0-87108-958-8
1. Mountain pine beetle--Rocky Mountains--Juvenile literature. I. Brooks, David, 1949- II. Title.

SB945.M78T87 2011
634.9'751560978--dc22

2011003286

Cover photograph by Carlye Calvin ©University Corporation for Atmospheric Research / Photo credits are on page 48.
Book design by Katie Jennings and Kay Turnbaugh / Printed in China

FOR ALL THE
FUTURE SCIENTISTS
—K.T.

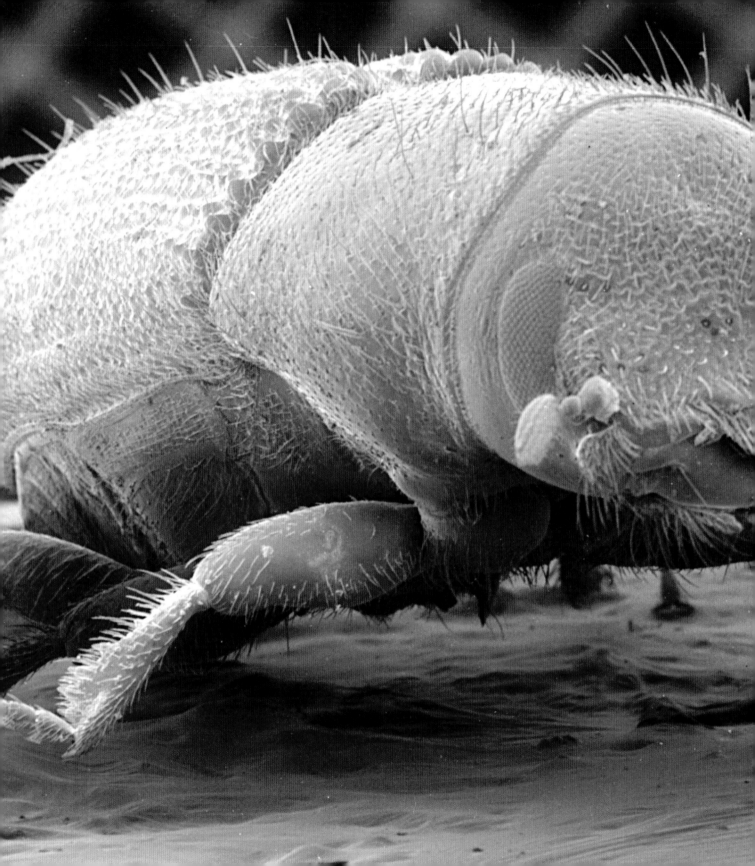

CONTENTS

TAKE A WALK THROUGH A FOREST IN THE ROCKY MOUNTAINS. Birds are twittering and fluttering overhead. Flowers of rainbow colors dot the ground under the trees.

The sun slants through the towering pines, showing off all their different colors of green. Some are blue-green, some are light green, some are really dark. The scent of pine is in the air.

Walk a little further. The pine tree smell gets more intense.

Ra-ta-ta, ra-ta-ta. Look up—you see a bird drilling into a tall tree, pulling off bits of bark with its strong beak and flinging them aside. The bird has made big bare spots on the tree's trunk.

The forest here isn't all green—some of it is gray and brown. Most of the dry, brown needles have fallen off the tree branches.

Walk even farther and you see that many of the trees have fallen over. They look like piles of sticks, stacked every-which-way.

What is happening here?

TINY BUT Mighty

Imagine an insect as small as a fat grain of rice killing a tree that towers 70 feet above the forest floor. That's as high as a seven-story building. It's as tall as the biggest dinosaur. Seems impossible, doesn't it?

Not when one mountain pine beetle joins forces with other mountain pine beetles. Together they form an army of mighty mountain pine beetles that can cause extreme damage to an entire forest.

Scientists named the mountain pine beetle *Dendroctonus ponderosae*. The Latin word *Dendroctonus* (den-DROCK-ton-us) means tree killer. It's a good name for the most destructive of the western bark beetles.

A BALANCING ACT

Mountain pine beetles have lived in the mountains forever. Even though they kill trees, they help the forests stay healthy. See the red-brown trees in the picture? Soon they will fall over and be recycled into the forest floor, making space for new trees.

For example, lodgepole pine trees are a favorite food for the mountain pine beetle. Old lodgepole forests are usually recycled through a big fire or by mountain pine beetles killing trees. When the old forest dies, it makes room for water, **nutrients,** and sunlight to reach young trees. The soil becomes more **fertile,** and new trees grow faster. Grass grows where it couldn't before and provides food for deer and elk.

7

LODGE-POLES

Native Americans from the Plains tribes needed about 15 poles to build a teepee. They traveled to the mountains to find the pine trees that grew the straightest and made the best lightweight poles. Today, we call those trees lodgepole pines.

The same trees were used for cross ties under the tracks of the early railroads that crossed the nation.

Today they are used for framing, paneling, posts, corral poles, utility poles, railroad ties, and pulpwood.

FOREST LIFE CYCLE

7. That helps new trees grow.

1. The old, unhealthy forest is attacked by...

6. and return nutrients to the soil.

2. fires and

5. provide wildlife habitat

3. mountain pine beetles.

4. The dead trees and fallen logs

This is a normal process. But in the 1930s and again in the 1970s, the beetles killed more trees than usual. **Droughts,** or long periods of time with little or no rain, made the trees weak and helpless to fight off beetle attacks. The mountain pine beetles ate through enormous forests, killing millions more pine trees than in a normal year. These severe attacks are called **epidemics**.

Today, the forests killed in the epidemics of the 1930s and the 1970s are green and healthy. But now there is a new mountain pine beetle epidemic. It's the worst yet.

The current epidemic has several causes.

🌲 For many years, humans have tried to stop forest fires, and that has created forests where all the trees are old. They are the perfect age for mountain pine beetle attacks.

🌲 As of 2008, the growing season in the West has grown longer by about two weeks, but the amount of rain has stayed the same. That means we've had a drought, which makes the trees more susceptible to attack.

🌲 The forests in the Rocky Mountains are now about 2 degrees warmer than during other beetle epidemics. Warmer winters at high altitudes have changed the beetles' life span from two years to one year, which means they are reproducing twice as fast.

🌲 The beetles can emerge any time from June to September. These new conditions mean the mountain pine beetles can grow in numbers and expand their range.

DOG HAIR THICKETS

Lodgepole pine trees usually grow on high mountain slopes above 6,000 feet. Their pinecones are sealed shut and need high temperatures like in a forest fire to open and release their seeds.

The average mature lodgepole pine tree is 2 feet wide and 70 feet high. They often grow very close together in dense stands called dog hair thickets. If you stand back, you can see that the thin, scraggly trees are packed so closely together that they look like dog hair.

9

Can you tell that we are in the middle of a mountain pine beetle epidemic?

You can clearly see the damage caused by the bark beetle when you hike in parts of the Rocky Mountains. Do you see big patches of brown trees? Mountain pine beetles have killed most of these trees. When you get closer you can see the smaller trees the beetles didn't kill and new baby trees hiding under the dead trees. In about ten years the new trees will be knee-to-waist high. Mountain pine beetles are helping start a new forest.

AN EPIC EPIDEMIC

The word epidemic usually describes an outbreak of disease. It also works to describe what's happening now with the mountain pine beetles.

In British Columbia, mountain pine beetles have killed trees on 33 million acres of lodgepole pine forest. That's about the size of the state of Alabama.

During this epidemic in the U.S., mountain pine beetles have killed 7 million acres of lodgepole pine trees. That's bigger than the state of Maryland.

Scientists predict that in the next fifteen years mountain pine beetles will kill another 22 million acres of trees. That would be an area equal to a third of the state of Colorado.

This map shows the range of the mountain pine beetle in the western parts of Canada and the U.S.

13

EXPONENTIAL GROWTH

The number of mountain pine beetles can get HUGE FAST.

Look at the mountain pine beetle family tree. At the bottom are the first female and male mountain pine beetles. The female lays 60 eggs. Not very many of them will survive and grow into adult beetles that can attack a new tree. Usually, only four eggs might live, but in an epidemic scientists estimate the survival rate might be as high as 10%. That means six of their offspring might survive.

Let's assume that half of those six are females, and they produce 60 eggs each. That's 180 eggs, and if 10% survive, that's 18 adult beetles. Just look how fast the numbers grow from there. By the fourth generation, there could be 162 adult beetles.

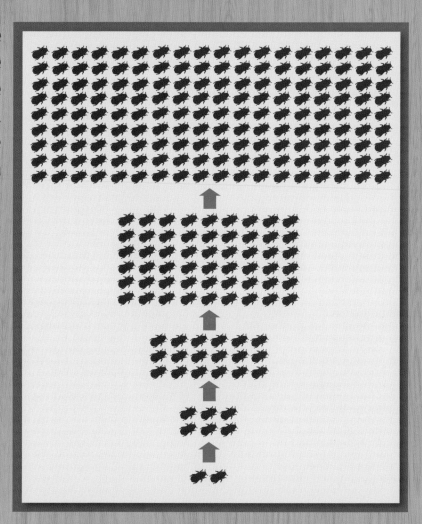

THIS KIND OF POPULATION GROWTH IS CALLED EXPONENTIAL GROWTH, BECAUSE THE NUMBER OF MOUNTAIN PINE BEETLES RISES AT A STEADY AND RAPID RATE.

BUILT FOR

BATTLE

The mountain pine beetle looks like a fat black grain of rice with wings and legs. Like all insects, the mountain pine beetle has three main body parts: the head, the thorax, and the abdomen. Each part helps this tiny warrior kill trees.

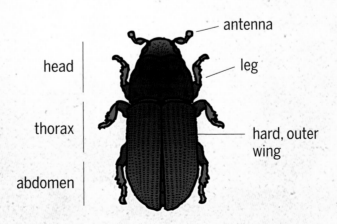

head

thorax

abdomen

antenna

leg

hard, outer wing

THE HEAD

Mountain pine beetles have many small eyes that together look like two big eyes. To them, the world looks like it does through a kaleidoscope. That limits their ability to find the perfect tree to attack by seeing it. Instead, they find a tree that's susceptible to attack by searching for its scent.

compound eye

antenna

mandibles

You might think they would use their nose to smell all the scents around them, but they don't. They use their two wire-like antennae that stick out from their heads to find the scent of a good tree to attack.

Once they land on a tree, they have to bore inside it. They have two sets of mouth parts. The first set is a pair of powerful pincers called mandibles. The mandibles don't move up and down like ours, but sideways, like scissors. Mountain pine beetles use their mandibles to grab and tear at the bark of the tree. Another set of finger-like appendages, called maxillae, move the food into the mountain pine beetle's mouth.

The mountain pine beetle's mandibles have microscopic pits, called mycangia, that are filled with fungi. Fungi are living microorganisms like mushrooms and mold, but these are too small to be seen with the human eye. The blue stain fungi carried by the mountain pine beetle helps it kill the tree.

THORAX

The thorax is the middle part of a beetle's body. It's where the wings and legs attach. The beetles have two sets of wings. Their hard wings protect their body as they crawl through the narrow tunnels they make in a tree's bark. The beetles raise their hard wings to fly, but they don't use them for flying. They have an extra, secret set of wings under the hard wings just for flying.

Once they land, mountain pine beetles use their six legs to walk around. Their back legs are designed to dig through wood.

ABDOMEN

The biggest part of the beetle is the abdomen. This is where it digests its food and where it breathes through tiny holes called spiracles.

This southern pine beetle has the same kind of wings as a mountain pine beetle.

The mountain pine beetle is much smaller than a penny.

SCENTS-R-US

Every tree has a unique scent. As a tree ages, its scent changes. Mountain pine beetles are attracted to the scent of old, weak trees.

Scientists think that mountain pine beetles might be attracted to areas where lots of trees are crowded together. Their combined scent is very alluring for a mountain pine beetle.

FINDING THE PERFECT HOME

As the female mountain pine beetle flies through the forest, she waves her antennae searching for the scent of a perfect home. She wants to find an old, big tree with thick bark that will help keep her offspring warm over the winter, just like a blanket. If she's lucky, she'll find a tree that is weak. A weak tree won't put up much of a fight when she chews through its bark.

The mountain pine beetle can fly as far as a mile searching for the perfect tree, so she needs a nice day for flying. She waits for a dry day when the temperature is over 60 degrees Fahrenheit. Usually she's flying about five or six feet off the ground. But sometimes she gets caught in a wind current, and she'll drift hundreds of miles above the trees. Most of the time, though, she's lazy and only flies as far as the next tree that will make a good home.

Once the female mountain pine beetle has found the perfect home, it's time to move in, but first she has to do a bit of remodeling. She has to make a hole through the tree's bark because there's no front door. How can such a tiny bug burrow into the thick, hard bark? Fortunately, she has just the right kind of jaws for the job. She uses her powerful mandibles to grab at the bark and tear it away. As she tunnels into the tree, she eats the tasty inner bark.

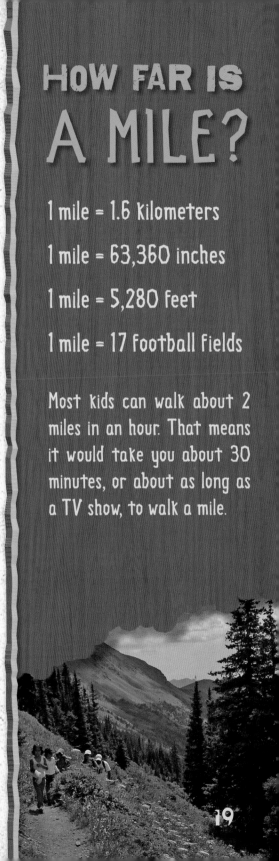

HOW FAR IS A MILE?

1 mile = 1.6 kilometers

1 mile = 63,360 inches

1 mile = 5,280 feet

1 mile = 17 football fields

Most kids can walk about 2 miles in an hour. That means it would take you about 30 minutes, or about as long as a TV show, to walk a mile.

BEETLE POOP

As the mountain pine beetle eats her way into the bark of a tree, she creates what is called boring dust or frass. Those are nice names for what it really is—beetle poop. It looks like fine sawdust, and it falls into crevices in the bark and around the base of the tree. Frass is one way to tell if beetles are attacking a tree and winning the battle.

THE TREE FIGHTS BACK

When a mountain pine beetle starts burrowing into the bark, the tree knows it is under attack. It fights back. It pumps sticky **sap** toward the beetle. In a successful counterattack the tree traps the beetle in its sap and ejects it through a small chute. This is called a pitch-out.

Sap can be white or yellow or pink, and a pitch-out looks like melted candle wax. If the tree is winning, you can see a dead beetle in the ooze.

Trees with pitch-outs look like they were sprayed with popcorn. Older pitch-outs are dry and crusty. If the tree is still fighting off the beetle, the pitch-out will be wet and sticky. If a tree is attacked by only one or two beetles and successfully pitches them out, it has a good chance of surviving.

21

THE PIONEER BEETLE

The first beetle to attack a tree is called the pioneer beetle. Once she starts tunneling into the tree, she sends out a scent to attract other beetles. She needs to invite lots of other beetles to her tree because it will take an army to kill the tree. Also, she needs a mate.

Once the mountain pine beetle has made her door, she continues to eat her way up the tree under the bark. She makes a tunnel, also called a gallery, where she lays her eggs.

Other mountain pine beetles arrive and begin burrowing under the tree's bark, where they too might find mates and lay their eggs. The neighborhood is growing.

When enough beetles have arrived to kill the tree, they send out a different scent that acts as a "No Vacancy" sign.

NO VACANCY

23

COORDINATED MASS Attacks

It's important that the pioneer beetle send out a signal scent to other beetles to help her attack a tree. Many beetles make it easier to overwhelm the tree, and they need to do it in three to four days or the tree will win. Once they lay their eggs, which will hatch into **larvae** in 10 to 14 days, those hundreds of beetle larvae will eat the tree's nutrient-carrying inner bark and kill the tree.

25

LIFE UNDER the BARK

After she finds a mate, the female mountain pine beetle moves her **frass** around in the **gallery**. She uses some of it to plug the hole she first made in the bark. For a while, the male helps her pack the frass down into the lower end of the egg gallery. When she's ready, the female mountain pine beetle lays her eggs.

By now, both the female and the male mountain pine beetles are nearing the end of their life. Soon after the female lays her eggs, both she and the male will probably die. But some of the parent beetles live through the winter. Scientists think that those might be the beetles that attack the tree at the end of summer.

The beetle's eggs are very small, about 1 millimeter across. They are pearly white. In about two weeks they hatch into larvae. The larvae are like short, fat worms. They don't have any legs, and their C-shaped bodies are soft. They are white, almost transparent, and they have little brown heads.

The larvae carve out their own galleries at right angles to the egg galleries. They do that by eating the inner bark of the tree.

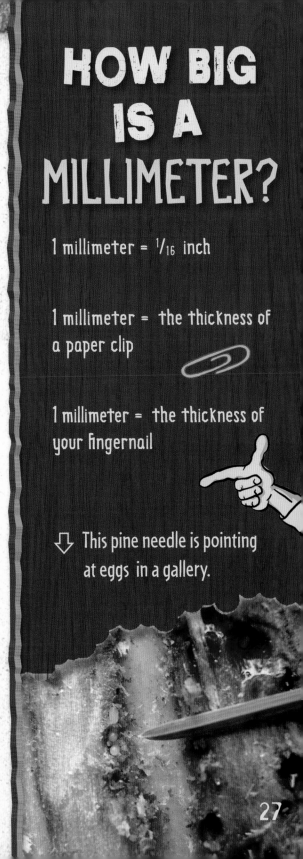

HOW BIG IS A MILLIMETER?

1 millimeter = $\frac{1}{16}$ inch

1 millimeter = the thickness of a paper clip

1 millimeter = the thickness of your fingernail

⬇ This pine needle is pointing at eggs in a gallery.

27

POP, CRUNCH, CHIRP
WHAT *IS* ALL THAT NOISE?

We can't hear it, but inside a tree it can get pretty noisy.

Start with the little POPPING sounds a tree makes when it dries out from lack of rain. Then, there are the CHOMPING, CRUNCHING, CRUSHING, CHEWING, and GRINDING sounds invading beetles make as they eat their way into the tree. To make matters even louder, the beetles talk to each other by CHIRPING.

To make their sounds, the beetles rub a scraper on their abdomen against a grooved surface on the underside of the left wing cover. It's like scraping a spoon against an old-fashioned washboard.

What are they saying? They chirp to each other to keep their galleries spaced apart so there will be enough food for everyone.

Scientists also think that female beetles are attracted by the male's regular, rhythmic chirps, which to them sound like little kisses. The males start to chirp when they enter the galleries that the females have made. They are letting the females know they have arrived. They are warning other males that the female in that part of the tree is taken.

Scientists have been studying how the beetles react to different sounds. Playing rock music through tiny speakers didn't bother the beetles. But when the scientists played digitally altered recordings of the sounds the beetles make, the beetles immediately stopped what they were doing. Some attacked each other, and some fled.

30

INSECT AntiFREEZE

Most of the one short year of a mountain pine beetle's life is spent as larvae, "chilling out" under the bark of a pine tree and waiting for spring. B-r-r-r-r! It's like living inside a freezer with the ice cream.

It would be easy to freeze to death because the mountain pine beetle's body is partly water. But mountain pine beetles have found a way to keep that from happening.

Amazingly, they change the carbohydrates in their bodies into alcohol, which acts like the antifreeze in your car. They don't need their **carbohydrates**—the starches and sugars that give them energy—in the winter. And since alcohol freezes at a much lower temperature than water, the mountain pine beetle larvae don't freeze to death. When warmer weather arrives, the larvae turn the alcohol back into carbohydrates. Now that they have survived the winter, the larvae need the carbohydrates for energy.

JUST LIKE A BUTTERFLY

After about 10 months, usually in June, the larvae dig oval cells in the bark where they turn into **pupae**. In July, the pupae transform into adult mountain pine beetles. They are ready to burrow out of their tree and fly to a new one where they will lay their own eggs.

A mountain pine beetle goes through a complete **metamorphosis** during its one-year life, just like a butterfly. The four stages are egg, larva, pupa, and adult.

BEETLE LIFE CYCLE

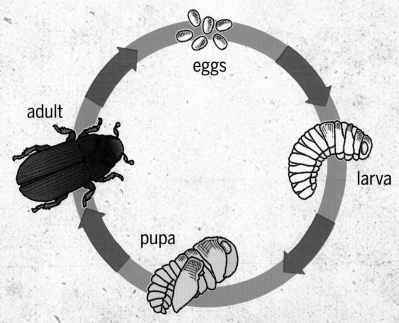

eggs

larva

pupa

adult

CALENDAR

JUNE–SEPTEMBER
Adult beetles emerge from trees, and in one to two days fly to new trees in search of a new home. The beetles burrow under the bark of the new tree and lay their eggs.

AUGUST–SEPTEMBER
The eggs hatch into larvae.

SEPTEMBER–JUNE
Larvae live through the winter under the bark of the tree.

MAY–JUNE
The larvae become pupae for two to four weeks.

JUNE–SEPTEMBER
The pupae become adult beetles and emerge from the tree.

IT'S A WAR in there

You might think that once the beetle burrows inside the bark of a tree, it will be safe from **predators**. Far from it. Lots of predators have found ways to get at the mountain pine beetles under the bark.

BIRDS

Small birds, like nuthatches, eat mountain pine beetles as they fly or as they start burrowing into the bark of a tree. Bigger birds, such as woodpeckers, find both the adult beetle and its larvae to be quite tasty. These birds hang onto the side of a tree and drill through the bark with their powerful beaks to get to the delicious beetles. Sometimes they take all the bark off the tree to get to the beetles.

WASPS

Parasitic wasps drill through the thin bark. They then sting, paralyze, and lay their eggs on the mountain pine beetle larvae. The wasp hatches, and the wasp larvae eat the live mountain pine beetle larvae.

PREDATOR BEETLES

The much larger larvae of other beetles like the round-headed woodborers also attack the mountain pine beetle larvae. Woodborer larvae can eat an entire gallery of mountain pine beetle larvae.

One of the mountain pine beetles' biggest enemies is the checkered beetle. An adult checkered beetle—which isn't much bigger than a mountain pine beetle—can eat 150 mountain pine beetles. The checkered beetle larvae can take over and live in the galleries of bark beetles and woodborers. A hungry checkered beetle larva can eat more than 100 young mountain pine beetles larvae.

A BLUE, BLUE FUNGUS

Mountain pine beetles' bodies have tiny grooves for carrying a deadly fungus—called blue stain fungus—into the tree. The fungi are deadly for the tree, but they are good for the beetles. The beetles are much healthier with the blue stain fungi.

inner bark (phloem) where the pine beetle lives

sapwood that is stained by the blue stain fungus

heartwood

outer bark

TREE TRUNK

The blue stain fungi also stick around the mountain pine beetle's mouth. As soon as the mountain pine beetle starts tearing at the bark to enter the tree, the fungi move from her mouth to the tree and begin to spread. The fungi plug up the parts of the tree that transport water and minerals. The fungus strangles the tree by making it hard for the tree to drink water. It stains the wood inside the tree blue.

Once the mountain pine beetle larvae hatch, they too eat the blue stain fungi. When the larvae become pupae and adults, the blue stain fungi will go with them to the next tree.

The blue-stained wood from trees that have been killed by mountain pine beetles is very distinctive and beautiful. It is used on walls in buildings and to make furniture.

THESE FUNGI ARE NOT FUN GUYS

The blue stain fungi (fungi is the plural form of fungus) are too small to see. Fungi are organisms that decompose and feed on dead organic matter, soil, poop, and other living things. Mushrooms are the most familiar example of fungi, and they also include molds, mildews, rusts, and yeasts. Many fungi help trees get water, but not the blue stain fungi. It actually works to keep the tree from drinking.

WHEN WILL it end?

Scientists are especially concerned about this current mountain pine beetle epidemic. The large number of old trees and the changes in the Earth's climate have changed the beetles' behaviors. In an epidemic, they attack any trees they can find. In our current epidemic, the beetles have been able to find lots of old, weak trees.

What happens if a fire starts in one of the huge **stands** of beetle-killed trees? Scientists guess that a fire like that could burn so hot it could bake the soil. The rain that falls on an area with baked soil cannot be absorbed by the soil. That can cause extreme **erosion** and mudslides. The muddy water that runs from these areas into lakes and streams could pollute the water that people drink.

Remember, mountain pine beetles are part of the normal life in the forest. Usually, predators, **parasites**, wet summers, and cold weather control their population. One of these might end this current epidemic, or eventually the beetles will run out of food.

Even though there are epidemics of mountain pine beetles, the beetles help the new trees and plants in the forest by killing off the old trees. As the dead trees decay, they provide nutrients for the new trees. Mountain pine beetles are part of healthy forests.

WE'RE STiLL LeARNiNG

Scientists are learning more about the mountain pine beetle every day. They are studying how it communicates, flies, and eats. They are especially interested in the blue stain fungus. They want to know more about how the mountain pine beetle carries the fungus from tree to tree and how it infects a tree. Some scientists are studying how the mountain pine beetle epidemic is affecting plants and animals in the forest.

Other scientists are measuring what pine trees release into the air. As the trees try to fight off the beetles, the scientists discovered that the trees release more particles and chemicals into the air. They think this makes the air quality worse, at least for a while.

DEAD TREES
MAKE MORE THAN
HOT AIR

When big parts of a forest die, the atmosphere around the forest can change. Beetle-killed forests can change how the clouds form and where it rains and snows for 10 years or more.

Beetle-killed trees release carbon dioxide or CO_2, which is the main greenhouse gas. Greenhouse gases make the Earth warmer. Computer models suggest that forests killed by mountain pine beetles can increase temperatures 2 to 4 degrees Fahrenheit for a short time.

Scientists also believe that when trees are threatened by beetles they release more particles and chemicals into the atmosphere to fight off the beetles. This can make the air quality worse.

WHAT'S A Kid to do?

What can you do to help? Here are some ideas.

🌲 Take part in a tree-planting project. Check with your local U.S. Forest Service, state forest service, or county extension office for opportunities in your area.

🌲 Become a scientist. We need to learn as much as we can about mountain pine beetles and what makes a forest healthy.

🌲 Do what you can to stop **global warming**. Do you recycle? Turn the lights out when you leave a room? Walk or ride your bike when you can? Everything you can do to stop global warming helps trees stay healthy.

🌲 And of course, be safe. If the weather is bad, especially if it's windy, look around. Are the trees dead? If so, there is a chance they could blow over, and it's time to get to a clear area.

43

GLOSSARY

carbohydrate — a biological compound that is a source of energy and food

drought — long period of time with little or no rain

epidemic — when something like disease spreads faster than normal

erosion — the gradual wearing away or transportation of soil or rock by water, wind, or ice

fertile — land that is rich in the nutrients needed for healthy plants and trees

frass — beetle poop

gallery — a tunnel made by an animal or a beetle

global warming — an increase in the world's temperatures

larva — a wingless, worm-shaped, immature insect (plural: larvae)

metamorphosis — a complete change in the form of an insect as it becomes an adult

nutrient — food or nourishment

parasite — a plant or animal that lives on or in another

predator — an animal or insect that kills other animals or insects to survive

pupa — an insect in the stage between larva and adult when it stops feeding and undergoes internal changes (plural: pupae)

sap (or pitch) — a thick fluid that circulates within a tree to distribute water and nutrients

stand — a group of trees growing together in one place

INDEX

Visit our website:
mpbbook.com

PHOTOGRAPHS